BAD DAD JOKES

Dad Jokes, Redneck Humor, Classic Vaudeville Skits and more!

JACK NORTON

CONTENTS

1

JOKES AND ONE LINERS

I'm from such a redneck town that we had us a beauty contest here in town a few years back and nobody won.

———

Our corn crop this year has been pretty slow...we only got 3 or 4 gallons per acre.

———

You know lots of our boys have been serving overseas and we are real proud of them. The average age of a solider from my redneck town is 57...we get fresh out of high school.

———

They consider a seven course meal a burger and a six pack where I come from.

———

Take my redneck neighbor Junior. He went to the dentist to have some wisdom teeth put in, but our dentist changed specialities...now he's a brain surgeon. That's cause his drill slipped. Poor Junior!

———

Yeah things have been a little strange around my town because for the first time ever there was actually a murder in our town. Such a small town this sort of thing never happens. It's a strange case too, has police baffled. See, they found the poor fellow that was killed in his own home, floating in his bathtub, and the bathtub was full of milk, and cheerios, and cut up bananas. Cops don't have too many leads, although they suspect a cereal killer!

Yeah our police department has been having a hard time lately. Someone actually broke in to their headquarters and robbed the place. Stole everything...why they even stole the toilets. Now the police don't have nothing to go on!

Boy, I'm sorry my jokes are so bad. My wife is always telling me how bad my jokes is, and I am sorry. I'm just a little slow. She's really the brains behind Pa. I might not be the sharpest tool in the shade, but I ain't dumb...just a little bit ignorant. But I'm proud of myself though. You know I've been working on a jigsaw puzzle for about 18 months now, and I just finished it! I am so proud...it only took me 18 months and the box said 3 to 5 years!

Why do cows wear bells?
Because their horns don't work!

How do you hide money from my redneck neighbor?

Place it under a soap dish.

———

My redneck neighbor finally went to a psychiatrist.

The doctor said "you're crazy."

My redneck neighbor said, "I want a second opinion."

The shrink said, "ok, you're ugly too!"

———

My redneck neighbor finally got married. On their honeymoon they were nearing Birmingham, Alabama and he put his hand on her knee. She started to giggle and said, "you can go further if you want to." So he drove up to Decatur.

Why did my redneck neighbor freeze to death?

Because he went to the drive-in movie to see "Closed For The Winter".

What do you call an alligator that's wearing a vest?

An investigator!

How do you make holy water?

Boil the hell out of it!

How did the big city hipster burn his tongue?

He drank his coffee before it was cool.

———

Did you hear about the new corduroy pillows?

They're making headlines everywhere!

———

What did the fish say when he swam into a wall?

Dam!

———

What kind of rooms have no walls?

Mushrooms!

———

There was a doctor in my redneck town who was discovered having relations with one of his patients! The scandal forced him to leave our town. It's a shame because he was the best veterinarian in the county!

———

What kind of shoes are made from banana skins?
Slippers!

———

What did the nut say when it was chasing the other nut?
I'm a cashew!

———

What do you get when you mix holy water and prune juice?

I think you get a religious movement.

______

Guess what happened when my redneck neighbor lost $50 to me on a TV football play?

I got him to lose another $50 on the instant replay!

______

Ever wonder who invented streaking?

It was my redneck neighbor when he mistook Ben Gay from Preparation H.

______

You know my redneck neighbors are a bit slow. It's really sad because they got pregnant and aren't too happy about it. The girl is considering getting an abortion because she doesn't think the baby is hers.

———

I once knew a girl who wore an anklet that said "Heaven's above".

———

I had a wife the last time I saw you. But her husband asked me to give her up.

———

I wrote this drinking song. Took me seven or eight years.

Just could never get past the first few bars.

———

How do you use a Hawaiian typewriter?
You just Waikiki, Waikiki, Waikiki...

———

How does the moon cut his hair?
Eclipse it!

———

Where does the General keep his armies?
Up his sleevies!

———

Politicians and diapers are a lot a like.

They should be changed, changed often, and for the same reasons.

———

I always bring an extra pair of socks with me when I go golfing.

In case I get a hole in one.

———

Why did the tomato blush?

Because he saw the salad dressing!

———

If someone dies and comes back as a hillbilly, is that reintarnation?

———

You know even though they talk about "peace and love", hippies can be awfully violent. Why I was just in the local food coop and a guy threw a bottle of Omega 3 at me.

Luckily my wounds were only super fish oil!

———

What do you get when you cross a joke with a rhetorical question?

———

I see by the papers up in New York theres a man gets hit by a car every 30 minutes.

Bet he's getting tired of that by now!

———

I crossed a sponge with a potato the other day.

Didn't taste good, but it sure did soak up a lot of gravy!

———

I crossed an elephant with a gopher. Wanna know what I got?

Some awfully big holes in the backyard!

———

What do you call a boomerang that does't come back?

A stick.

———

Mahatma Gandhi, as you know, walked barefoot most of the time, which produced an impressive set of calluses on his feet. He also ate very little, which made him rather frail and with his odd diet, he suffered from bad breath.

This made him "A Super-Calloused Fragile Mystic Hexed By Halitosis"!

———

Viagra shipment stolen!

Cops are looking for a gang of hardened criminals.

———

How do you get to be a good wood carver?

Whittle by whittle.

———

Why can't a bike stand up by itself?

It's two tired.

———

Some no good man come along and cut off all the tails on my cows. It's just terrible! You know what I'm going to have to do now? I'm going to have sell them all wholesale now. You may be asking yourself "why wholesale"?

Well, the answer is simple: I can't re-tail them!

———

Do you remember the chemical formula for water? If not, I'll tell you. It's: H, I, J, K, L, M, N, O.

I know this cause my teacher said it was H to O.

———

Why did the physics teacher break up with the biology teacher?

There was no chemistry.

———

My redneck neighbor came home the other day and shot his dog.

When I expressed my surprise he said: "someone called me and said my wife was fooling around with my best friend."

———

My redneck neighbor decided to drive to Nashville, Tennessee to see his cousin. About twenty miles from his destination he saw a sign that said "Nashville Left". So he turned around and drove back home to Alabama.

———

My poor ol' dad died last year when my family couldn't remember his blood type in time for the paramedics to give him a blood transfusion. As he was dying he kept shouting, "be positive", but it's hard to do that without him here.

———

How does my redneck neighbor spell "farm"?
E-I-E-I-O.

———

What did that rapper fella Jay Z call his girlfriend before they got married?
Feyoncé!

My redneck neighbor was brought to the hospital with severe facial burns.

Seems he had been bobbing for french fries again.

———

Guess how my redneck neighbor broke his leg at the golf course?

He fell off the ball washer.

———

My redneck neighbor from the North was reading the Bible for the first time and called me to talk about it.

He said, "it says a lot about Saint Paul - but there's nothing in it about Minneapolis!"

———

My redneck neighbor noticed his car being stolen.
So he chased it down the street trying to copy down the license number.

———

Some people might call us hillbillies, but we prefer the kinder term, Mountain Williams.

———

How do I feel when there is no coffee?
Depresso.

———

The Three Rings of Life:

1. Engagement Ring
2. Wedding Ring
3. Suffering!

———

What keeps rock stars cool?
    Their fans!

———

Why couldn't the lifeguard rescue the hippy?
    He was too far out, man!

———

If you have a large gathering of sad pitbulls is that considered a pity party?

———

Did you hear about the restaurant on the moon?

Great food, no atmosphere.

———

Did you hear about the police department that couldn't solve the case of their stolen toilets?

Cops have nothing to go on!

———

What did the beaver say to the oak tree?

It was nice gnawing you!

———

Struck up a conversation with a spider today. Seems nice. He's a web designer.

1st Beatnik: How do you get to Carnegie Hall?

2nd Beatnik: Practice, man, practice!

How many tickles does it take to make an octopus laugh?

Ten-tickles!

---

5 Year Old Daughter: Mom, why is some of your hair white?

Mother: (Smiles). Every time you make me sad, another hair turns white.

5 Year Old Daughter: (Wide Eyes). Wow, mom! What did you do to Grandma?!

———

Why didn't they play cards on the Ark?
Because Noah was always standing on the deck.

———

Women are a lot like a guitar. They both come with strings attached.

———

Magician: I can make anything disappear.
Tom: (Holding Cup) Do it to my tea.
Magician: (Waves Hand) Done!
om: (Holding Cup) It didn't work.

———

Owl: Pretty cool having an owl drive your Uber, huh?

Me: Please face the front.

———

I lost my job at the bank on my very first day. A man asked me to check his balance, so I pushed him over.

———

What do you call a fake noodle?

An Impasta.

———

What do you call cheese by itself?

Provolone!!

———

What do you call a fish with no eyes?
    Fsh.

———

What kind of computer can sing?
    A Dell!

———

Wife: Now I know why they call you Pa. Because you're pathetic!
    Husband: And I know why they call you Ma. Because you're always riding ma' ass!

———

You: Wanna go to yoga?
    Me: I'm down, dog!

———

She: "What do you do in your free time?"

He: "I stalk."

She: "Really? I enjoy walks in the park or go to the movies with friends."

He: "I know."

———

2

HOLIDAY JOKES: HALLOWEEN

Why are graveyards so noisy?
Because of all the coffin!

———

What does a vampire never order at a restaurant?
A stake sandwich.

———

Why did Dracula get thrown out of the haunted house?

He was a pain in the neck!

———

Why didn't the mummy have any friends?

He was too wrapped up in himself.

———

What happened to the cannibal who was late to dinner?

They gave her the cold shoulder!

———

What is a witch's favorite subject in school?

Spelling.

———

What happened to the guy who couldn't keep up payments to his exorcist?

He was repossessed.

———

Why are demons and ghouls always together?

Because demons are a ghoul's best friend!

———

Why did the headless horseman start a business?

He wanted to get ahead in life.

———

Where do movie stars go on
Halloween?
Mali-boo!

———

What do Italians eat on Halloween?
Fetticini Afraid-o.

———

Why don't skeletons ever go trick-or-
treating?
They don't have any body to go out
with.

———

3

HOLIDAY JOKES: THANKSGIVING

Why did the farmer run a steamroller over his potato field on Thanksgiving Day?

He wanted to raise mashed potatoes.

———

Who doesn't eat on Thanksgiving?

A turkey because it is always stuffed.

———

What do you call a turkey on the day after Thanksgiving?
Lucky.

———

Why can't you take a turkey to church?
They use FOWL language.

———

What do you get when you cross a turkey with a banjo?
A turkey that can pluck itself!

———

My editor just told me to stop writing these Thanksgiving jokes, but I told him I couldn't quit "cold turkey".

———

4

HOLIDAY JOKES: CHRISTMAS

What's the difference between a snow-man and a snow-woman?
Snow-balls!

———

Why did Santa's little helper feel depressed?
He had low elf esteem!

———

December is always a hard time for me because of my claustrophobia.

You know, my fear of Santa Claus!

———

Jiminy Christmas! I was hanging Christmas lights the other day and I fell of a thirty foot ladder! Don't worry, though, I'm ok.

Luckily for me I was just on the first step!

———

Did you hear about what happened to the dyslexic devil worshipper on Christmas Day?

He sold his soul to Santa.

———

What kind of motorcycle does Santa ride?

A Holly Davidson.

———

What kind of cars do elves drive?

Toy-otas.

———

What do you call a bankrupt Santa?

Saint Nickel-less.

———

Why are Christmas trees so bad at knitting?

They always drop their needles.

———

What did the beaver say to the Christmas tree?

Nice gnawing you.

———

What do you call Santa's most impolite reindeer?

RUDEolph!

———

What do you call Santa's helpers?

Subordinate clauses.

———

What do you call a kid who doesn't believe in Santa?

A rebel without a Claus.

———

What did Santa give his depressed elf friend for Christmas?
An elf help book!

———

What do you get when Santa accidentally goes down a chimney when the fire's lit?
Krisp Kringle.

———

What do snowmen call their kids?
Chill-dren.

———

Why did Frosty the Snowman want a divorce?
His wife was a total flake.

VAUDEVILLE SKIT: NO NEWS, OR WHAT KILLED YOUR DOG

Land sakes friends, there ain't been too much goings on down in my redneck hometown lately, no sir. 'Cept for my cousin-in-law Naybob. Now ol' Naybob he's married to my wife's sister Beuladine, and let me tell you somethin', I don't know how he manages. In fact, he seldom do. 'Cause just last month he was gettin' all mixed up, and his Doctor told him he outta get a way from town for a few weeks and just go up in them mountains for a rest, you know, to relax.

Needed to get his head cleared. He went home and told all the members of our family, and he asked me to watch over his affairs while he was away. He said, "Buddy, while I'm away I don't wish to be annoyed by any letters or telegrams, in fact, I don't wanna receive any news of any kind."

So he went away and was gone about three or four weeks. We come back to our town very much improved in health and very anxious about some news from home. Naybob got offa the train at the depot, and came up to me and said...

"Well Buddy, how is everything at home? Is there any news?"

· · ·

I said, "no boy, there ain't no news...ain't nothing been happenin' 'round here while you was away. Everything's just about the same."

"Nothing happened?" he asked.

"No, hoss, ain't nothin' happenin', there ain't no news."

He said, "Buddy, I'm just dying for some word from home, now, please tell me any old shred of news. Tell me any little thing, don't matter how trifflin', just tell me somethin'."

"Well, Naybob, there ain't no news, nothin' to tell you...excepten for one little thing...since you've been away, yer dawg died."

He says, "my dawg died, eeeh? Well that's too bad...what do you suppose killed my dawg?"

"Well Naybob," I says, "yer dawg ated some burnt horse meat and that's what killed yer dawg."

"He eated burnt horse meat? Where did he get burnt horse meat to eat?"

"Well Naybob, yer barn burned down and after the fire had cooled off, the dawg went in and eated some of the burnt horses, and we thinks thats what killed the dawg."

He says, "my burn burned down, eeh?"

"Yup, yup sho did, yer barn done burned down."

"Buddy, how did the barn catch fire?"

"Well Bob, see the sparks from the house blew over and caught on to the barn, and the barn done burned down, and burned up all them cows and horses and mules and after that fire done cooled off, yer dawg went inside the barn and eated some of that burned up horse meat and we thinks that's what killed yer dawg."

He says, "My house burned down too?"

"Yup, yeah, yes yer house, why it's completely and totally destroyed."

Of course he wanted to know how the house caughted on fire.

"Well, Naybob, they had some candles burning in the house, and one of them candles caught on to the curtains, and the curtains caught on to the roof, a spark flew over and caughted on to the barn and burned the barn down and that burned up all the cows and horses and mules, and after that fire done cooled off, yer dawg went inside the barn and eated some of that burned up horse meat and we thinks that's what killed yer dawg."

He said, "they had candle burning in my house where I have gas and electricity? Why I didn't never know there was a single candle in the place!"

So I says, "yes sir, yes sir, they had all the candles there they had a ton of can-dles burning all around the coffin."

"The coffin?!" he says, "whose dead?"

. . .

"Oh yeah, Naybob, that's another little thing what am I forgot to tell you about. Since you've been away your mother in law died!"

"Oh my mother-in-law died, eeeh?" Naybob said very gleefully.

"Yeah she am mostly certainly dead all right, no need to worry bout that no more. We had her buried, cremated and embalmed, just to be on the safe side."

"Well what killed my mother-in-law?" he asked.

"Well, Naybob," I says, "I don't know exactly what killed her, but everybody in town thinks that it was the shock of your wife running off with your best friend! But other than that, there's been no news. No news at all."

ABOUT THE AUTHOR

Jack and Kitty Norton are Emmy Award winning and Amazon bestselling authors. Married high school sweethearts, the duo runs a publishing company based in Minneapolis, Minnesota.

Kitty's 2018 memoir, *The Unbecoming*, was an Amazon Best Seller for four weeks. The niece of reggae legend Bunny Wailer (of Bob Marley and the Wailers fame), Kitty had found success while still in high school as a session vocalist at Prince's Paisley Park Studios, and was signed to a recording contract before she graduated. What looked to be a promising career in pop music was cut short by a debilitating car accident. Bedridden for over a year, the former cheerleader and model had ballooned to 515 pounds. *The Unbecoming* documents how this disabled, stay-at-home, self-employed, and depressed lady lost 345 pounds...completely naturally: without any gimmicks, surgeries, pills or fad diets.

In 2019, the Jack and Kitty Norton released a memoir called *Two Stalkers One Goal*. In a story stranger than fiction, the inspiring book offers hope and healing for victims of stalking, cyber-stalking, narcissistic abuse, gossip and bullying...all with more twists and turns than any Hollywood thriller.

Jack's latest book, *Cornstars: Rube Music In Swing Time*, is a sweeping over-view of American musical entertain-ment set in the later days of minstrelsy through the early days of television. It was nominated for the 2021 Association for Recorded Sound Collections Awards for Excellence in Historical Recorded Sound Research.

Earlier in their career, Jack and Kitty co-created, co-directed, co-wrote and co-starred in *The Zinghoppers Show*, a children's television series which earned six regional Emmy Award nominations for Nashville Public Television and was broadcast on over 150 PBS member stations nationwide and in 175 countries on the AFN Family Channel and on Trinity Broadcast Network. Four original songs written and performed by Jack and Kitty Norton were featured in the Oscar nominated Willem Dafoe film *The Florida Project* (A24) by director Sean Baker (Tangerine) which debuted at the 49th edition of Cannes Directors' Fortnight as part of the Cannes Film Festival.

Connect with Jack at:

http://www.jackandkitty.com
http://www.
instagram.com/jacknortonbooks
http://www.
twitter.com/jacknortonbooks

 twitter.com/jacknortonbooks

 instagram.com/jacknortonbooks

DISCLAIMER

All rights reserved.

No part of this book may be used or reproduced in any manner whatsoever without written permission from the authors, except in the case of brief quotations used for review purposes.

This is a work of fiction. Names, characters, places and incidents are solely the product of the author's imagination and/or are used fictitiously. Any resemblance to actual persons, living or dead, organizations, actual events or locales is entirely coincidental. The author acknowledges the trademark status of products referred to in this book and acknowledges that trademarks have been used without permission.

All attempts have been made to verify the information in this book. However, neither the authors nor the publisher assumes any responsibility for errors, omissions, or contrary interpretations of the content within.

Do you research before posting anything online. This information is intended for entertainment use, consists of opinions, and should not be constructed as legal advice or business guidance. Neither the authors nor the publisher can be responsible for any content that you choose to post online nor loss of income. Again, this book is for entertainment purposes only, and so the views of the authors should not be taken as expert instructions or commands. The reader is responsible for his or her own actions. Adherence to all applicable laws, including but not limited to international, federal, state and local regulations is the sole responsibility of the purchaser or reader.

This book may contain reference links to other relevant content. Neither the authors nor the publisher can be responsible for content posted on other sites.

Neither the authors nor the publisher assumes any responsibility or liability on behalf of the purchaser or reader of this book.

Thank you to all my friends that connected with me on JackAndKitty.com - you gave me the push I needed to write this book. And thank you to my best friend and soulmate, Kitty. I'll love you forever and beyond.